FOREWORD

Welcome to the Spring 2011 edition of the Stability Operations Lessons Learned and Information Management System (SOLLIMS) Lessons Learned "Sampler". The general structure of the "Sampler" includes (1) an **Introduction** that provides an operational or doctrinal perspective for the content, (2) the Sampler **"Quick Look"** that provides a short description of the topics included within the Sampler and a link to the full text, (3) the primary, topic/issue-focused Stability Operations (SO)-related **Lessons Learned report***, and (4) links to **additional reports or other references** that are either related to the "focus" topic or that address current, real-world, SO-related challenges.

This lessons-learned compendium contains just a sample – thus the title of "sampler" – of the observations, insights, and lessons related to **Fighting Corruption** available in the SOLLIMS data repository. These observations are worth sharing with military commanders and their staffs, as well as civilian practitioners with a Stability Operations-related mission / function – those currently deployed into conflict environments, those planning to deploy, the institutional Army, policy makers and other international civilian and military leaders at the national and theater level.

Lessons Format. Each lesson is provided in the form of an Observation and Recommendation (O&R). The "O & R" follows a standard format:

- Title (Topic)
- Observation
- Discussion
- Recommendation
- Implications
- Event Description

Occasionally you may see a "Comments" section. This is used by the author of the "O&R" or a Lesson Manager to provide additional personal perspective or to identify related references on the Observation. The "Event Description" section provides context for the Observation in that it identifies the source or event from which the content was developed.

You will also note that a number is displayed in parentheses next to the title of each lesson / observation. This number is hyper-linked to the actual O&R within the SOLLIMS database; click on the highlighted O&R number to display the O&R entry and access any attachments (references, images, files) that are included within SOLLIMS for this O&R. **Note, you must have an account and be logged into SOLLIMS in order to display the SOLLIMS data entry and access / download attachments.**

If you have not registered on SOLLIMS, the links in the reports will take you to the login or the registration page. Take a few short minutes to register for an account in order to take advantage of the many features of SOLLIMS and to access the stability operations related products referenced in the report. We encourage you to take the time now to provide us with your perspective as related to a single observation / lesson in this report, or to the overall value of this "Sampler" as a reference or guide for you and your unit/organization and staff. **By using the "Perspectives" text entry box that is found at the end of each O&R – seen when you open the O&R in your browser – you can enter your own personal comments and observations on this O&R.** We welcome your input. We encourage you to become a regular contributor to the SOLLIMS Community of Interest !!!

>>>>|<<<<

At PKSOI we continually strive to improve the services and products we provide the global stability operations community. We invite you to use our web site at [http://pksoi.army.mil] and the many functions of the SOLLIMS online environment [http://sollims.pksoi.org] to help us identify issues and resolve problems – we welcome your comments and insights.

---

*All reports in the "Sampler" are generated by the SOLLIMS Lessons Report Builder tool.

Judges, police, and corrections department members discuss problems and solutions during rule of law conference in Jalalabad, Afghanistan. (Photo by Jennifer Cohen, U.S. Army)

INTRODUCTION

Welcome to the Spring 2011 edition of the Peacekeeping and Stability Operations Institute (PKSOI) Lessons Learned "Sampler". The focus for this edition is on **Fighting Corruption**.

> *"Corruption can undermine effective statebuilding in post-conflict settings. The legitimacy and effectiveness of the state can be severely impeded by corrupt practices, thereby reducing public trust and diminishing the capacity of the state to function effectively."*
>
> *(Fighting Corruption in Countries Rebuilding after Conflict, USAID, November 2008)*

Corruption – the abuse of entrusted authority for private gain – can be particularly nefarious in post-conflict reconstruction settings. Post-conflict reconstruction situations are normally characterized by large-scale injections of resources. If legal and institutional frameworks are weak, fragile, or non-existent – which they often are – and if expertise to manage/track such resources is also lacking, the stage is set for corruption. In such circumstances, corrupt practices can quickly take root and expand.

Corruption is not just a Governance issue; it is a multi-sectoral problem. It encompasses Security Sector Reform, Justice/Legal Reform, Economic Stabilization & Reconstruction, and Transition. Altghouth a country may have laws and regulations in place that address corrupt practices, its mechanisms for detection, enforcement, and judicial action may be weak or non-existent – necessitating security sector and legal reforms. Also, an absence of financial controls, performance monitoring, transparency, and accountability over contract funds and reconstruction money may exacerbate incidents of corruption – requiring governance, legal, and reconstruction-related actions.

Corruption is also multi-level problem. It is found at all levels of government – from central to regional to local levels. At the higher levels of government, instances of grand corruption may occur, involving higher-level officials and larger sums of money: embezzlement, kickbacks, campaign finance irregularities, political patronage, and clientelism. At the lower levels, administrative corruption may surface in the form of everyday, low-level abuse of power by local officials: bribes, gifts, speed money, and influence peddling – adversely affecting service delivery to the public. Hence, corruption can easily impact all levels of society.

Anti-corruption relates to the laws and administrative procedures for accountability and transparency – across government institutions and in the private sector. It relates to processes whereby organizations can monitor the government's behavior – from initial interventions to the establishment of a maintainable host nation capacity to perform the same. Anti-corruption also includes protections for the monitoring organizations.

Development of a comprehensive, multi-sector **anti-corruption strategy** is essential in the fight against corruption in a post-conflict environment, due to its often weak or fragile institutional frameworks.

The business of developing an anti-corruption strategy may include:

- identifying and assessing the causes and vulnerabilities for corruption
- establishing reliable government/public finance systems for budgeting, procurement, and tax administration
- strengthening legal frameworks, procedures, and ethics
- creating accountability and tracking mechanisms – both within and outside government
- working closely with donors on accountability and transparency
- training civil servants on anti-corruption
- addressing and monitoring the delivery of government services

Through such anti-corruption mechanisms, practices, and cadres, post-conflict countries have a far greater chance of curbing corruption, gaining stability, and achieving economic and social development than otherwise.

To win the fight against corruption, it is imperative that civilian and military Stability Ops planners/practitioners, donor staffs, and host nation officials work together to develop, implement, and coordinate appropriate anti-corruption practices and actions, and that they commit to monitor this effort over time.

Table of Contents

Related References / Links

U.S. Army Peacekeeping and Stability Operations Institute (PKSOI)	
Director	COL Cliff Crofford
Deputy Director	COL John Bessler
Chief, Publications & Knowledge Management Division	COL Rory Radovich
Chief, Lessons Learned Branch	Dan French
Lessons Learned Analyst	Dave Mosinski

Unless otherwise stated, whenever the masculine or feminine gender is used, both are intended.

Disclaimer: All content in this document to include any publications provided through digital attachment is considered unclassified, for open access. This compendium contains no restriction on sharing / distribution within the public domain. Existing research and publishing norms and formats should be used when citing "Sampler" content and any publications provided.

Sampler "Quick Look" – FIGHTING CORRUPTION

Click on [Read More ...] **to go to Sampler topic.**

- The United Nations Development Programme (UNDP) can play a significant role in the fight against corruption in a conflict-affected state. [Read More ...]

- One way to fight corruption in a post-conflict country is to establish "common ground" between the government, citizens, and civil society - namely "access to information." [Read More ...]

- According to a regional subject matter expert, among the grievances, "anger against government corruption" was the most deep-rooted grievance that drove people into revolution. [Read More ...]

- With regard to the presence of corruption, known and perceived corruption of Afghan officials was a central theme among local communities and local officials during the 2004-2008 timeframe. [Read More ...]

- Leadership and strategic planning have been noticeably absent in efforts to develop the civilian court system in Afghanistan, and this shortfall has adversely impacted rule of law. [Read More ...]

- Police and military forces are the first line of defense against corruption, but they can also engage in corrupt practices. [Read More ...]

- Strengthening public servants' knowledge, ethics, skills, networks and attitudes is key, because it is through public servants that government services are planned and delivered, critical innovations conceived and realized, needed reforms carried out and trust in government restored. [Read More ...]

- The rule of law and control of corruption are at the centerpiece for successfully addressing challenges in social, economic, and political development. [Read More ...]

Peacekeeping and Stability Operations Institute
US Army War College
22 Ashburn Drive, Upton Hall
Carlisle Barracks, PA 17013

11 Apr 2011

Subject: SOLLIMS REPORT – FIGHTING CORRUPTION

1. GENERAL

Anti-corruption relates to laws and administrative procedures for accountability and transparency – across government institutions and in the private sector – and to processes whereby organizations can monitor government behavior – from initial interventions to the establishment of a maintainable host nation capacity to perform the same. Anti-corruption also includes protections for the monitoring organizations.

Anti-corruption is a complex and challenging business. In the post-conflict environment, it is absolutely critical for civilian and military Stability Ops planners/practitioners, donor staffs, and host nation officials to work together to develop, implement, and coordinate anti-corruption practices and actions – so that corruption is not allowed to take root, expand, and undermine governance.

This report contains related observations, insights, and lessons currently available within the SOLLIMS knowledge base.

2. OBSERVATIONS & RECOMMENDATIONS

a. Topic. Afghanistan: UNDP Interventions to Combat Corruption (732)

Observation.

The United Nations Development Programme (UNDP) can play a significant role in the fight against corruption in a conflict-affected state. In the case of Afghanistan, the UNDP has been able to influence key donor groups and host nation authorities and gain long-term commitments for combating corruption. Much work remains to be done; however, the UNDP's attention to building consensus, identifying causes of corruption, targeting key host nation stakeholders for supporting anti-corruption efforts, and then guiding development of anti-corruption strategic plans are key components in the complex process of fighting corruption - in a country where it has become a major threat to governance and state-building.

Discussion.

Through UNDP's initiative in 2006, an initial informal donor group was established to address the subject of fighting corruption in Afghanistan. That donor group consisted of the World Bank, Asian Development Bank (ADB), Norway, Sweden, the European Union, and the United Nations Office on Drugs and Crime (UNDOC). The group worked throughout 2006-2007 to achieve the following:

- developed inputs/recommendations on anti-corruption issues for Afghan national-level policy.
- developed an Anti-Corruption Road Map - published in April 2007. This road map consisted of a comprehensive assessment of corruption in Afghanistan and recommendations on how to more effectively fight it.
- sent a joint letter to the Afghan government's chairman of the Joint Coordination Monitoring Board to express unease with the leadership of the GIACC (General Independent Administration for Anti-Corruption, established by President Karzai in December 2003).

Of note, the group conducted various Vulnerability to Corruption Assessments (VCAs), addressing the types, causes, impact, and extent of corruption. The prevalent types of corruption identified were: petty corruption, bribery, extortion, theft of government assets, patronage, and corruption in government procurement. The principal causes of corruption in Afghanistan were assessed as:

- The opium economy. Counter-narcotics efforts provide opportunities for corrupt officials within the security and justice sectors, particularly at the provincial and lower levels, to extort enormous bribes from drug traffickers.
- Large inflows of international assistance, combined with the pressure to spend these funds quickly, and insufficient oversight and accountability.
- Inadequate systems to detect, prosecute, and punish corrupt practices - owing primarily to a weak justice sector. The judiciary does not have any communications infrastructure, file management system, or libraries, it lacks facilities and equipment, and judicial staffs lack skilled professionals. The level of corruption in the judicial system is reported to be quite high.
- Patronage networks. In the Afghan culture/tradition of kinships, those in privileged positions (from senior officials to lower level civil servants) often employ corrupt practices to expand power and extract profits to provide favors/benefits to relatives.

With regard to the impact/extent of corruption in Afghanistan, it was unquestionably damaging to both Afghan governmental legitimacy and state-building efforts. A survey conducted in 2006 across 13 provinces found that 60 percent of Afghans considered the Karzai government to be the most corrupt the country had experienced in 50 years. Respondents indicated that well over 50% of government services commonly sought required some sort of corrupt practice: water services, power services, release of goods through customs, vehicle registrations, license plates, drivers licenses, identity cards, marriage certificates, passports, medical services, school services, etc. The most common practice of corrupt behavior was civil servants delaying delivery of services until a bribe had been paid.

In January 2007, UNDP launched the Accountability and Transparency (ACT) project. At that point in time, there had been no clear Afghan government counterparts/champions in the field of "anti-corruption." Few concrete steps had been taken by international agencies, donors, or the Afghan government to address corruption issues. UNDP decided to anchor its approach in the Ministry of Finance, building an alliance with officials in this ministry. Here it prepared the groundwork for more comprehensive and long-term, strategic anti-corruption efforts. UNDP initially helped that office with developing anti-corruption agendas and internal monitoring systems.

Building upon its alliance in the Ministry of Finance, UNDP scheduled a 3-day stakeholder workshop - bringing together some one hundred participants from other government institutions, as well as from the international community. Subsequent this conference, the Afghan government announced the establishment of a new anti-corruption body: the High Office of Oversight and Anti-corruption (HOO).

In August 2008, HOO was officially established - with a respected senior administrator as its head. HOO's charter was to implement a national anti-corruption strategy, take lead on corruption prevention and awareness, and coordinate government-wide efforts to fight corruption. The UNDP provided support to HOO's senior management in developing the organizational structure. The UNDP facilitated an exchange with the Indonesian government to provide expertise to HOO on the formulation of a "strategic plan." In 2009, UNDP provided support to HOO in crafting a new Anti-Corruption Law that better defined HOO's mandate, covering the following: corruption prevention, public awareness, proper management of public affairs, and simplification of processes and procedures in government offices dealing with the public on a regular basis.

Through the assistance of the UNDP, HOO completed its "Anti-Corruption Strategic Plan: 2011 - 2013," which was published in December 2010.

Other successes of UNDP's ACT program include the following:

- Establishment of a Fraud Investigation Unit in the Ministry of Finance.
- Establishment of a "grants facility" to build a watchdog capability of civil society actors and the media. Three organizations were initially supported

with watchdog training: the Saba Media Organization, Integrity Watch Afghanistan, and Integrated Approach to Community Development.
- Collaboration with the Civil Service Commission to integrate ethics and anti-corruption training in the leadership training program for high-level Afghan civil servants.
- Establishment of a Complaints Office in the Ministry of Finance.
- Development of action plans for several ministries and sectors to strengthen processes/procedures to preclude corrupt practices: the Ministry of Finance, the Civil Service, the road sector, and the energy sector.

Based on the anti-corruption successes/achievements in Afghanistan cited above, the following "specific lessons learned" are offered in the report "Fighting Corruption in Post-Conflict and Recovery Situations: Learning from the Past," UNDP, June 2010:

- Political will is of critical importance in moving the anti-corruption agenda forward.
- Know the context. If a project is developed without fully taking into account the political context, UNDP's efforts will never succeed.
- Projects need to be realistic; it is easy to be overambitious with anti-corruption projects. When formulating projects, one should consider what is feasible to achieve, given the circumstances of the country, and build in sufficient buffers to allow for delays.
- The projects need to be focused. There is so much that needs to be invested in moving one activity forward, that if a project has too wide a focus and too many partners, it will be difficult to manage the reform process.
- Donors and agencies need to work together in a coordinated manner. In post-conflict situations with a heavy donor presence, it is also important to link the political and technical levels. Unless there is also a push at the political level for anti-corruption, those working at the technical level will not be successful.
- A single anti-corruption project is not sufficient. UNDP (and the UN family) should build in anti-corruption components and leverage other existing projects and programs, where relevant, in the fight against corruption.

However, UNDP's successes/achievements represent only a fraction of what needs to be done in Afghanistan with regard to fighting corruption. As stated earlier in this discussion, corruption has become rampant across Afghanistan, affecting the everyday life of citizens - from obtaining electricity services, to applying for drivers licenses, to participating in a court hearing, to competing for a business contract.

An area critical to anti-corruption efforts that has not been adequately addressed/reformed is the civilian justice sector. The existing systems for prosecuting and punishing corrupt practices are woefully inadequate. The Afghan judiciary is viewed as the most dysfunctional and corrupt institution in all of Afghanistan. With most judges in the provinces earning $35-50 per month, corruption in the court system has been characterized as "endemic," as judges take bribes to supplement their inadequate incomes. It is commonplace for a person approaching a courthouse to be intercepted by persons with some link to the judge who will inquire as to the problem and then solicit a bribe. Judicial integrity is lacking. Only about 12% of judges have a university degree, and only about 57% have completed any judicial training prior to their appointment. The Afghan Supreme Court has not developed a strategy or plan of action to address shortfalls. The judicial system is not staffed, equipped, trained, or inclined to properly handle cases of corruption. Non-state institutions - 'loyal jirgas' and 'shuras' - are a potential avenue for delivering justice; however, they are highly patriarchal and use practices in violation of the Afghan Constitution and human rights principles.

Recommendation.

1. Organizations and donors engaged in stability operations should develop an anti-corruption road map / strategy at the very outset. A holistic approach should be taken, bringing together all major donors and all appropriate host nation institutions. The UNDP should be leveraged, if mandated/engaged in the host nation. Primary causes of corruption in the host nation should be identified, assessed, and addressed. Accountability and tracking mechanisms should be imperatives for all development funds and contracts. Pressures to spend funds quickly should be eliminated.

2. Organizations engaged in stability operations should consider incorporating the following tact taken by UNDP: create a core group of stakeholders within the host nation to serve as the cornerstone for anti-corruption efforts. Build alliances and expand to other ministries/sectors.

3. Since corruption has permeated all levels of governance across all of Afghanistan, and since the people of Afghanistan have voiced dissatisfaction about corrupt practices in routine service delivery, organizations engaged in stability operations should conduct information operations to tell the populace what is being done about corruption. The UNDP's "grants facility" was one effort in this direction, where three media groups were trained/supported to provide overwatch and report on corruption; however, much more needs to be done in this regard.

4. Organizations engaged in stability operations should ensure that comprehensive judicial reforms are conducted in parallel with anti-corruption efforts. It is recommended that the Afghan Supreme Court be engaged to formulate a national plan of action to strengthen integrity in the judiciary, including training in judicial ethics, and to take initiative in developing wide scale

reform measures. Extending judicial reforms out to non-state institutions - 'loya jirgas' and 'shuras' - should be examined, with the goal of shaping a more accountable and standardized, traditional justice system. Salaries for judges need to be addressed/increased to allow them to make a living solely through their work, vice corrupt practices.

Implication.

If an anti-corruption strategy is not developed from the outset, if key stakeholders within the host nation government are not co-opted from the outset, and if the judicial system is not reformed to handle cases of corruption, then a climate of corruption may rapidly develop -especially as external aid pours in to the host nation and opportunities for corruption are expanded.

Comments.

A related document is the "Anti-Corruption Strategic Plan: 2011 - 2013," developed by the High Office of Oversight and Anti-corruption (HOO), Islamic Republic of Afghanistan, December 2010.

A related O&R which discusses the absence of leadership & strategic planning in civilian legal reform in Afghanistan, and which recommends that the U.S. State Department step up to lead Afghan rule of law initiatives [and, in the interim, either the International Security Assistance Force (ISAF) or the Combined Join Interagency Task Force (CJIATF) could fulfill this role as a "bridge to the future"] is O&R 710.

A related O&R which discusses the impact of corruption on governance (in Afghanistan), and which recommends development of an information operations campaign to tell the population what is being done about corruption, is O&R 713.

A related O&R which discusses anti-corruption tools (in Sierra Leone and Liberia), and which recommends building alliances from within the host nation government, is O&R 731.

Event Description.

This observation is based on the report "Fighting Corruption in Post-Conflict and Recovery Situations: Learning from the Past," United Nations Development Programme (UNDP), June 2010.

Return to
"Quick Look"

b. Topic. Fighting Corruption - The "Common Ground" Approach (<u>731</u>)

Observation.

One way to fight corruption in a post-conflict country is to establish "common ground" between the government, citizens, and civil society - namely "access to information." "Access to information" - credible and timely public information - can establish the foundation for an informed, active citizenry to hold public officials accountable for the allocation, utilization, and management of resources. This has been the philosophy of an international non-governmental organization (NGO) called Search for Common Ground (SFCG), which has worked to promote the proper functioning of government & society in Sierra Leone and Liberia. SFCG's experience in these two post-conflict countries indicates that success can be gained by utilizing a "common ground" approach. It also offers tools and guiding principles for institutions & individuals working anti-corruption efforts in other post-conflict environments.

Discussion.

Elections in post-conflict Sierra Leone and Liberia, in 2004 and 2005 respectively, raised high expectations among citizens for responsive governance, rapid economic development, and improved service delivery. The inability of government officials to meet those expectations, however, soon resulted in perceptions & accusations by the public of corrupt practices among government officials - some of which were validated.

Pre-conflict, these two countries possessed political frameworks in which power and political authority were heavily centralized within the executive branch. Executive branch officials had unchecked access to state funds and resources, which they often used to enhance a patron-client political system of favors, bribes, etc. and which became a source of conflict. The unregulated and mismanaged extraction of natural resources by these officials, as well as by warlords and combatants, was also a cause/driver of persistent conflict. In post-conflict Sierra Leone and Liberia, recovering from such circumstances, the NGO SFCG employed a "common ground" approach to educate citizenry about what state officials were doing with regard to funds, resources, and projects. It did so in a non-confrontational manner that had the buy-in of many state officials.

One tool employed by SFCG was "Accountability Now" - a radio program which improved communication between government officials and their constituents around the topics of financial management and service delivery. In Sierra Leone, even though new laws required local government councils to publish their income and expenditure statements, most local councils failed to comply with them. This failure (deliberate in nature) bred mistrust between councils & citizens and fueled perceptions of corruption among communities. The "Accountability Now" radio program addressed this issue by publicly disseminating information on the income and expenditures of local councils, by presenting financial statements on development projects, and by including commentary/participation from government officials and independent analysts. Armed with information obtained through these radio broadcasts, civil society groups could then follow up by visiting development sites to see whether the announced expenditures actually matched activity and outputs. In some cases, corruption was exposed, and unfit public officials were terminated. Overall, "Accountability Now" facilitated discussion between citizens and government officials (via radio call-in), put pressure on local government councils to explain actions and improve their performance, and resulted in more accountable and transparent behavior.

A second tool employed by SFCG was town-hall meetings, which provided a forum for discussion - bringing together law-makers, local authorities, civil society groups, and citizens. These meetings were not designed to be "name and shame" meetings. It was emphasized before and during meetings that civil society has a role in positively encouraging government officials toward behavior of transparency and accountability. Prior to meetings, the facilitators (from SFCG) met with panelists (many of which were government officials) to ensure that the format and agenda fit the interests and needs of the forum/community. These pre-meetings helped to ensure that town-hall meetings were seen as non-threatening and would be used as a positive forum for dialogue. In Sierra Leone, for example, town hall meetings often centered on service-related agendas (food provision, water supply projects, road improvements, etc.). Meetings brought women, youth group, and civil society leaders face-to-face with government officials from multiple levels to engage on the status of these services. Every meeting covered the actions plans and priorities of the government offices, including the reading of their financial statements. Meetings were broadcast live via radio to provide even more "common ground."

A third tool employed by SFCG was similar to the other two in that it helped establish "common ground" and made use of information operations (IO); however, it was different in that it was "outside the box" of traditional information dissemination. SFCG actually created a radio "soap opera." Its purpose was to appeal to the general public through entertainment (and it reached government officials as well!) to make them aware of appropriate behaviors and of consequences for corrupt practices. In Liberia, SFCG's radio soap opera was called "Today Is Not Tomorrow (TNT)." One storyline depicted a negative character using his political connections and wealth to mismanage the community's development funds. As the story went on, a community audit report discovers that he has embezzled a large sum of money, he goes to court, and he ends up with a 10-year sentence. Also, positive characters and scenes are portrayed in the program - displaying honesty, accountability, and transparency of fund management, and offering new models of behavior and leadership. Sometimes, the radio soap opera used satire to bring humor to sensitive subjects/issues. As a proof of success, a wide survey among listeners was conducted, and most participants stated that they had gained an understanding of corruption dynamics and how to engage with/within communities on these matters.

Overall, the use of the "common ground" approach by SFCG in Sierra Leone and Liberia proved to be very effective in the fight against corruption. Along with the three tools mentioned above, SCFG also applied certain "principles" to guide its anti-corruption interventions in these post-conflict countries. Those principles were:

- Manage expectations. SFCG conveyed to the public that there are significant challenges and complexities in executing anti-corruption interventions. In so doing, the public no longer expected instantaneous change and instead realized that it will take time, and their cooperation, to root out corruption, change mindsets, and establish appropriate procedures and behaviors.
- Maintain neutrality. SFCG did not take sides / did not favor any political party, any certain government council/office, any certain ethnic or societal group. By maintaining neutrality, SFCG was able to bring diverse actors together in a number of forums to talk about sensitive issues related to, or having potential for, corruption.
- Create the "demand side" of governance. SFCG sought to build a critical mass of diverse actors with the requisite skills to "demand" better governance and accountability. For example, SFCG would bring numerous civil society group leaders to town-hall meetings to dialogue with government officials on their financial reports and service delivery.
- Build alliances from within. Within the government system/structure, there are always some individuals who want change for the greater good and will work for it. SFCG sought out those individuals and then leveraged them for critical information and for taking the lead on actions, whereby SFCG could then maintain its neutral status.
- Be gender inclusive. SFCG was careful to report equally on the involvement of both men and women in corrupt practices. Likewise, the voice/input of women on issues dealing with corruption was given equal weight to the voice/input of men. SFCG achieved success in allowing both men and women to participate equally in radio and town-hall sessions covering governance and corruption issues.

Recommendation.

The following actions are recommended for fighting corruption in post-conflict countries:

1. Use a "common ground" approach for dealing with corruption in a post-conflict state. Work (hard) with government officials to promote "access to information" for their constituents. "Access to information" - credible and timely public information - would establish the foundation for an informed, active citizenry to

hold public officials accountable for the allocation, utilization, and management of resources.

2. Designate an organization to serve as a facilitator for executing the "common ground" approach, along the lines of SFCG in Sierra Leone and Liberia. The designated facilitator should take note of certain guiding principles that served SFCG well. Those are: Manage expectations, maintain neutrality, create the "demand side" of governance, build alliances from within, and be gender-inclusive.

3. Use media tools, especially community radio programs, to improve communication between the government and its constituents on topics/issues dealing with development, service delivery, management/utilization of funds, etc.

4. Hold town-hall meetings on a regular basis, to provide an open forum on topics/issues dealing with development, service delivery, management/utilization of funds, etc. Ensure they are non-confrontational. Include officials from multiple levels of government, if feasible. Appropriate agendas, ground-rules, security measures, etc. must be set well in advance of such meetings.

5. Develop innovative actions within the realm of information operations that could have wide appeal to the public, such as the radio soap operas in Liberia, to broaden awareness about corruption scenarios and appropriate consequences. Every country is unique with regard to its societal groups, norms, mindsets, etc. Consider tools, technologies, and venues that would best reach the target audiences in the given country/society/environment.

6. Consider development of an Information Operations (IO) campaign to combat corruption, incorporating recommendations 1 through 5 above.

Implication.

A "common ground" approach implies that the cooperation of state officials can be garnered - i.e., their willingness to provide budgetary information & status' on development projects and also their willingness to participate in forums with local citizens. Convincing government officials that their long-term political survival depends on participatory and accountable leadership may require a shift in mind-set. This may take considerable time and energy.

If "common ground" is not established between government and constituents in a post-conflict state, then the use of resources/funds by state officials may go unchecked (unless other measures are established), actual and perceived corruption is likely to increase, governance and rule of law will suffer, and citizens may turn elsewhere for service delivery and justice.

Comments.

A related O&R which discusses the impact of corruption on governance (in Afghanistan), and which recommends development of an information operations campaign to tell the population what is being done about corruption, is O&R 713.

Event Description.

This observation is based on the article "Battling corruption in the search for peace: The Common Ground Approach," by Oscar Bloh and Ambrose James, in New Routes, Vol. 14, No. 3-4, 2009.

Return to "Quick Look"

c. Topic. Post-Revolutionary Transitions (714)

Observation.

Revolutions in the Middle East and North Africa over the past several months contain driving factors and dynamics not previously seen in such processes. The "Post-Revolutionary Transition" conference, held at the National Defense University (NDU), Washington D.C., examined theories and processes of revolution, factors for successful post-revolution transition, and the role of the military - with a focus on recent events in the Middle East and North Africa. The conference was co-sponsored by the Institute for National Security Studies (INSS) and the United States Institute for Peace (USIP).

Discussion.

Recent Middle East and North African cases, particularly Egypt's revolution of Jan-Feb 2011, provide key insights on the changing dynamics of revolution and on post-revolutionary transition.

Social networking and revolution. In recent revolutions, social networking and video sharing websites (SNS/VSS) played a great role to rapidly and widely influence public opinion, organize opposition/protest, and drive people to join a revolution. Networks with those websites propagated information with remarkable speed. People in the networks tended to respond instantly without deep-thinking, and this group behavior accelerated and expanded the revolution. Numbers of young military officers were involved in on-line activities and subsequently influenced the military's stance.

Military role. Military response is one of the keys to conclude a revolution - democratically and less-violently, or not. In Egypt, the military was reluctant to open fire on crowds, and this behavior facilitated peaceful political transition. According to an Egyptian guest speaker, what caused the military to support revolution-minded people included:

- long and strong relationships between citizens and military personnel
- public opinion, especially its influence via the internet

Revolution drivers in Egypt. Long time autocratic governance, poverty, rampant unemployment, etc have been pointed out as the people's grievances behind this revolution. According to a regional subject matter expert, among the grievances "anger against government corruption" was the most deep-rooted grievance that drove people into revolution.

Factors for successful transition. As a result of comparative studies, the following were presented as factors for successful post-revolutionary transition:

- The revolution is relatively peaceful, and the revolution/opposition is well-organized
- The revolution/opposition is not dominated by radical/anti-democratic factors
- The military agrees to the establishment of civilian rule and to remain intact, and it has the support of the population
- The new government distances itself from the old regime, can deliver basic services, and can stabilize the economy
- Civil society forms political parties and associations to sustain the new government
- A process for future peaceful transitions of government is put into place
- External actors provide positive support at critical moments
- The establishment of a Truce & Reconciliation Commission
- The presence of a functional and credible judiciary

Recommendation.

Lessons learned, especially with respect to revolution dynamics and revolution's changing nature - as seen in recent revolution cases - should be studied for USG stability and reconstruction operations, as well as for engagement policy in this region.

Implication.

As some countries have potential for revolutions in the near future and revolutions tend to expand much faster than ever, the failure to take timely and appropriate actions may have implications for the course/outcome of the revolution. Likewise, in countries where the USG is implementing stability and reconstruction operations, there are potential adverse implications if revolutionary drivers (corruption, poor governance, poverty, rampant unemployment, etc.) are not monitored and acted upon.

Event Description.

This observation is based on the "Post-Revolutionary Transitions" conference, National Defense University, 14 March 2011.

Return to "Quick Look"

d. **Topic.** **Obstacles to Local Governance - Insights from Eastern Afghanistan** (713)

Observation.

Building local governance in a "conflict-affected" state can be a slow, difficult process. In Eastern Afghanistan, local governance efforts made only marginal progress over the 2004-2008 timeframe, with the driving factors proving to be: the level of security vis-a-vis the insurgent threat, the availability of civil servants, the level of corruption among government officials, the country's hold-over system for the administration of local governance, and the availability of resources (both coalition and host nation) for dedicating to local governance efforts.

Discussion.

Building local governance in eastern Afghanistan during the 2004-2008 timeframe was one of three major efforts, or "pillars", in the counterinsurgency strategy of Regional Command-East, with the other two being security and development assistance. Security - building up the Afghan National Army and the Afghan National Police and conducting operations against various insurgent groups - was Regional Command-East's priority effort and received the greatest resources. Development assistance - improving roads, schools, health clinics, irrigation systems and working with Afghan groups/institutions supporting such projects - also received considerable resources. Local governance was a distant third, receiving the lowest level of resourcing.

Challenges to counterinsurgency and stability operations - in general - were: the size of the area of operations, rugged terrain, harsh winters, the lack of transportation infrastructure, and societal complexities in this unstable/tribal state. O&R 678 speaks to this latter challenge - where the central government is weak, tribal actors strong, local groups set in their ways, and violence pervasive.

During this timeframe (2004-2008), the primary factors specifically affecting local governance efforts in eastern Afghanistan were: the level of security vis-a-vis the insurgent threat, the availability of host nation civil servants, the presence of corruption, the hold-over system for the administration of local governance, and the availability of resources for local governance efforts.

With regard to **the level of security and the insurgent threat**, extending local governance to certain areas of eastern Afghanistan was highly problematic, if not impossible, given the availability of military resources to provide security and to deal with insurgent threats. British forces deployed to Helmand Province were continuously engaged by Taliban forces, particularly when they established a presence in the vicinity of district governance facilities. Coalition forces operating in the Bermel district of Paktika Province experienced numerous major attacks, and insurgents twice overran the district government facilities. In parts of Kunar and Nuristan Provinces, particularly in the Pesh, Korangal, and Waygal valleys, localized insurgencies were very strong, threatening firebases and specifically targeting and hindering the growth of local governance. In contrast, where security conditions were favorable, or at least adequate, local governance efforts were able to make headway and improve over time. 2nd Battalion/27th Infantry significantly influenced security conditions in Paktika Province by deploying groups of soldiers to district government centers for weeks at a time, providing enough security for the nascent district governments to take root. In Nangarhar Province, where security conditions became very favorable by 2008, district-level governance was able to expand markedly, owing much to the dedicated efforts of the Jalalabad Provincial Reconstruction Team (PRT) and a special troops battalion which conducted security operations in support of governance. Also, as the host nation's security forces were built and trained over time, those assets were used increasingly to help provide security for governance, but that process was slow to develop over the 2004-2008 timeframe.

With regard to **the availability of host nation civil servants**, the huge shortfall/absence of civil servants severely impeded local governance efforts. Decades of war had significantly reduced the pool of civil servants in eastern Afghanistan, most of whom had migrated to Pakistan or other countries. Security risks, hardship, and low pay were the contributing factors in their failure to return to their former districts and municipalities in Afghanistan. Compounding the problem were major deficiencies in governmental infrastructure. In 2004, most governors occupied physical "compounds", but they lacked basic equipment and supplies. At the district level, conditions were worse. Over the 2004-2008 timeframe, recruiting and training of civil servants in eastern Afghanistan was almost non-existent. One of the very first efforts to address this problem was an initiative by the government of India, in 2008, to recruit and train 500 civil servants.

With regard to **the presence of corruption**, known and perceived corruption of Afghan officials was a central theme among local communities and local officials during the 2004-2008 timeframe. Corrupt governors were one of the biggest obstacles. Mullahs, business groups, and provincial councils publicly and privately accused provincial governors of corruption. These corrupt provincial governors appointed many of the district governors (at the level beneath them), even though by law they were not charged to do so. Many district governors then lacked legitimacy and were reactive with regard to handling problems in their districts, rather than being proactive with their communities in planning projects and priorities. Many Afghan citizens expected coalition forces to end the wide scale corruption among provincial and district officials. In spite of several efforts by Defense and State Department personnel to confront provincial officials with charges of corruption when there was compelling evidence, not enough progress was made in this regard.

With regard to **the existing, hold-over system for administration of local governance**, in eastern Afghanistan (actually in most of Afghanistan) the hold-over system lacked legitimacy in the eyes of local citizens. Elections were held in September 2005 to choose provincial council members, but no elections were scheduled for the lower levels of governance - district and municipality. The Ministry of Interior (MoI) had been responsible for overseeing/administering sub-national governance, but it had acquired a reputation for corruption and inefficiency. To rectify the problem, in August 2007, President Karzai issued a decree establishing the Independent Directorate for Local Governance (IDLG), with the mandate to:

> "consolidate and stabilize, achieve development and equitable economic growth, and to achieve improvements in service delivery through just, democratic processes and institutions of governance at the sub-national level, thus improving the quality of life of Afghan citizens."

IDLG officers began an ambitious program to overhaul governance at the provincial, district, and municipal levels. They asserted themselves as "supervisors" of local officials. They became involved in interactions, meetings, and projects between coalition PRTs and local governments. They improved the coordination among national ministries in Kabul having connections to local governance. In April 2008, with the support of international advisors, IDLG officers developed a "Five Year Strategic Work Plan" which outlined goals for policy development, institution building, and governance, along with entry points where donors could provide financial and technical assistance. Also, the IDLG examined various ways to devolve power from Kabul out to the provinces to give provincial officials greater budgetary and policy authority.

With regard to **the availability of resources for governance efforts**, there were significant shortfalls both within the Afghan government and within the coalition forces for dedicating to local governance efforts. With respect to coalition forces, there were not enough civilian or military political advisors /

pol-mil officers to meet the requirements of building local governance in the many provinces, districts, and municipalities of eastern Afghanistan. Due to their limited numbers, political advisors concentrated their efforts at the provincial level - with less contact and engagement at the district and municipal levels. It was not until 2009 that the U.S. Embassy in Kabul posted officers at the district level in eastern Afghanistan. With respect to the Afghan government's resources, host nation funds and transportation resources to support local governance initiatives were very inadequate. In early 2008, the IDLG approached the international community to establish a "governor's fund" for governance initiatives. With regard to transportation shortfalls, coalition forces and PRTs helped arranged access to helicopters and aircraft to get new IDLG personnel transported to remote provinces (such as Badghis and Zabul), where dozens of provincial leaders, provincial council members, tribal leaders, and other local leaders would be assembled for discussions on governance, security, and development.

The above discussion presents only a snapshot of the many obstacles to building local governance in eastern Afghanistan during the 2004-2008 timeframe, where coalition forces made marginal progress in this regard. Nonetheless, it was commendable progress - considering the resources at their disposal and the highly demanding, complex environment in which they were operating.

Recommendation.

1. Building local governance cannot progress without having security / a secure environment. Security highly depends on the cooperation of local groups. Coalition forces should strive to gain a comprehensive understanding of local groups during planning for operations. Human Terrain System (HTS) assessments, such as "Local Governance in Rural Afghanistan," should be developed as early as possible. Coalition forces should also develop a comprehensive engagement strategy to gain the influence/support of local groups. Beyond efforts to establish a secure environment, the sustainment of security will ultimately depend on building the capacity of the host nation's security forces. Much progress has been made lately in Afghan capacity-building, as discussed in O&R 712.

2. Building local governance cannot move forward without civil servants. If there has been an exodus of civil servants, efforts should be made to draw them back to the host country. Adequate security and sufficient pay must be addressed. Additionally, to fill any void, coalition forces should work with the host nation government to recruit and train local citizens to become civil servants. The establishment of regional civil service academies should be considered.

3. Building local governance requires taking action on cases of corruption. All military and civilian personnel involved in stability operations should receive pre-deployment training on corruption, along with periodic reminders about corruption

awareness and reporting. Coalition forces should conduct an information campaign to tell the population what is being done about corruption.

4. Building local governance should not ignore the existing, hold-over system for administration of local governance. It should be examined and revised, as appropriate. Programs like the ILDG should be developed and implemented as early as possible. Likewise, district-level elections should be planned and conducted as early as possible.

5. Building local governance requires adequate resourcing, especially in the personnel arena. Coalition forces should be resourced with appropriate numbers of political advisors / pol-mil officers to cover the local communities in their areas of operation - as determined through pre-deployment plans and assessments.

Implication.

If a secure environment is not established, then local governance efforts simply cannot make progress. Moreover, if the civil servant cadre is largely absent and not rebuilt, and if coalition forces do not have sufficient political advisors to work with them, then local governance efforts will be severely handicapped and slow to develop. Significantly long-term engagement will be required to overcome these shortfalls.

Comments.

A related article which provides a baseline guide on local communities and governance in eastern and southern Afghanistan is "Local Governance in Rural Afghanistan," by Human Terrain System (HTS) - Afghanistan, ISAF Headquarters - Kabul, 26 October 2010.

A related O&R which addresses the importance of incorporating local engagement into the planning process for stability operations is O&R 669.

A related O&R which discusses challenges to stabilization efforts in an unstable/tribal state such as Afghanistan - where the central government is weak, tribal actors strong, local groups set in their ways, and violence pervasive - is O&R 678.

A related O&R which cites the importance of re-building a cadre of public servants for post-conflict countries is O&R 603.

A related O&R which discusses the importance of building the capacity of host nation security forces and their ministries is O&R 712.

A related O&R which cites one organization's strategy for engaging communities (Iraq context) is O&R 709.

Event Description.

This observation is based on the article "Local Governance and COIN in Eastern Afghanistan 2004-2008," by Robert E. Kemp, MILITARY REVIEW, January-February 2011.

Return to "Quick Look"

e. Topic. Leadership and Strategic Planning for Rule of Law – Afghanistan (710)

Observation.

Leadership and **strategic planning** have been noticeably absent in efforts to develop the **civilian** court system in Afghanistan, and this shortfall has adversely impacted rule of law. Conversely, leadership and strategic planning have been hallmarks in development of the **military** court system in Afghanistan - resulting in significant progress for rule of law for the Afghan National Army (ANA). These two attributes of military legal reform in Afghanistan - leadership and strategic planning - may have application toward development of the civilian court system in Afghanistan, as well as in other operations/countries.

Discussion.

Despite years of efforts by an array of organizations and governments, the proper dispensation of justice throughout Afghanistan remains elusive. According to a Kandahar Province Survey Report conducted in March 2010, 67 percent of the Kandahar population believes that the Afghan government has been unable to provide justice because of its corruption; however, 53 percent of the Kandahar population believes that the Taliban are "incorruptible."

One of the more promising areas of legal reform has been within the Afghan military. The ANA's judicial system now includes functioning courts, judges, prosecutors, defense counsel, and appellate review. The ANA's judicial system has full capacity for pretrial detention and for long-term post-trial confinement. From Sep 2007 to Sep 2010, the ANA was able to adjudicate approximately 400 cases each year.

Success of the ANA's judicial system can be attributed, in part, to the leadership and strategic planning provide by the Combined Security Transition Command-Afghanistan (CTSC-A). Through an organized and unified command and control scheme, the ANA legal system has been guided by focused, well-resourced international advisors. Three full-time CTSC-A advisors have been dedicated to the ANA General Staff Legal Department in Kabul. Outside Kabul, the NATO

Intermediate Joint Command, in cooperation with CTSC-A, has provided U.S. and coalition military judge advocates to advise ANA prosecutors, defense attorneys, and judges at each of the ANA corps headquarters. As part of its strategy for legal reform, CTSC-A has also dedicated hundreds of military and contract advisors who provide training and mentoring for counterparts in Afghanistan's Ministries of Defense and the Interior.

In contrast to CTSC-A's efficient relations with the ANA, the development of Afghanistan's civilian court system has lacked both a primary leader and a systematically applied strategy. Civilian agencies have continuously struggled for a "patchwork of consensus." Coordination meetings, with few accountability mechanisms, have been substituted for efficient, accountable leadership. Rule of law initiatives on the civilian side are not managed by the U.S. Government's responsible agency (the Department of State), but rather, they are carried out by a host of federal agencies whose staffs are in Kabul, but who work outside the purview of the U.S. Ambassador. These many U.S. federal agencies, not to mention the many donor governments and non-governmental organizations, have not established any central mechanism to coordinate and oversee activities with regard to rule of law.

Without central ownership or planning for rule of law activities, the Afghan courts have suffered from persistent corruption. Low pay for judges and prosecutors has practically institutionalized this corruption. These officials commonly take bribes to earn a subsistence living. The key institution that should connect the police and the prisons - namely, the court system - has not been professionally developed. The Afghan civilian court system lacks competent and honest prosecutors to lead investigations. The Afghan civilian court system remains very Kabul-centric, with few attorneys dispatched to rural areas to establish a representation of law and order.

On a positive note, a recent State Department decision to establish a rule of law-related Combined Joint Interagency Task Force (CJIATF) is a step in the right direction. Task Force 435, which provides corrections oversight of the national security detention facilities, in partnership with the Afghan National Security Forces, is expanding into a CJIATF and could provide (if so developed) some command and control with regard to the civilian court system.

As it stands, however, no single leading U.S. agency has stepped up to oversee all facets of the rule of law in Afghanistan. Until one does, either ISAF or the CJIATF could be tapped as a "bridge to the future."

Recommendation.

1. A single entity, namely, the U.S. State Department, should step up to oversee all facets of the rule of law in U.S. stability interventions such as Afghanistan. It is imperative that one single entity take responsibility and accountability for leading rule of law initiatives and for training, mentoring, and partnering with the Host Nation's legal institutions/actors.

2. Until the U.S. State Department does take the lead on rule of law activities in Afghanistan, two viable "bridges to the future" would be: (1) ISAF or (2) the CJIATF. ISAF has nationwide reach through its subordinate command and control structures: the NATO Training Mission-Afghanistan and the Intermediate Joint Command. Its inherent leadership, security, training program, international teaming, and Host Nation partnering ability could significantly impact legal reforms on the civilian side across the breadth of the country. CJIATF, given senior civilian and military leaders accountable to both the U.S. Ambassador and to the president of Afghanistan, could likewise influence and develop rule of law institutions nationwide - working from the corrections systems and linked to the courts, the police forces, and the Ministries of Justice and the Interior.

3. Afghan judges and prosecutors need to be paid adequately - to combat bribery and corruption.

4. For international efforts/contributions to the rule of law, the Government of Afghanistan and the United Nations should take steps to ensure that donors' efforts are aligned with the Host Nation's legal reforms/priorities, per the Afghan National Development Strategy.

Implication.

If no single U.S. agency takes the lead in overseeing all facets of the rule of law in U.S. stability interventions such as Afghanistan, with accountable leadership and an overall strategy for developing and mentoring host nation entities, then the civilian courts in those environments will continue to languish and be ineffective. Citizens may then look elsewhere to obtain justice.

Comments.

A related article which discusses the lack of faith/trust that the Kandahar population has for the district and national governments and for their dispensation of justice is "Human Terrain System: Kandahar Province Survey Report - March 2010," by Glevum Associates, March 2010.

Event Description.

This observation is based on the article, "Establishing Rule of Law in Afghanistan: A Patchwork Strategy of Consensus," by Mark R. Hagerott, Thomas J. Umberg, and Joseph A. Jackson, in Joint Force Quarterly (JFQ), Issue 59, 4th Quarter 2010.

Return to
"Quick Look"

f. Topic. Security Sector Reform (SSR) Must Recognize that Corruption is a Major Challenge (606)

Observation.

Police and military forces are the first line of defense against corruption, but they can also engage in corrupt practices. The seminar "Fighting Corruption in Security Sector Reform (SSR)" focused on how corruption can undermine confidence in government and enable criminal elements to gain advantages. Efforts to reform the security sector must recognize that corruption is a major inhibitor to reform, and programs must be developed to deal with it accordingly. Several SSR experts articulated thoughts on best practices for dealing with corruption.

Discussion.

Curbing corruption in the security sector is now seen as one of the major program elements of SSR. The international community has come to recognize that high corruption levels in a country can facilitate international trafficking of drugs, arms, or human beings; money laundering; and, subsequent terror financing. In addition, corruption was acknowledged to be one of the basic impediments to economic growth. SSR programs need to enforce transparency and accountability; however, more specific recommendations are elusive. Exact policies, steps, or measures for SSR are not easily defined, largely due to the peculiar nature of the problems and social conditions in different countries.

Compounding this problem is the ambiguity of / around the definition of the security sector itself, as organizations are usually included in the sector if they are related to security in any way (directly or indirectly). They can include: criminal justice organizations (police, judiciary, etc.); management and oversight bodies (executive and legislative branches, municipal legislatures, etc.); military and intelligence services (armed forces, paramilitary forces, border guards, etc.); and even non-core institutions (customs and other uniformed bodies).

Speakers revealed that corruption in the security sector can be especially negative in terms of its influence on development. Corruption impedes investment, and it creates an unstable economic environment and physical insecurity of investors. Corruption establishes informal rules, to which all actors engaged in the shadow economy abide - which begets informal protection from the side of law enforcement in exchange for bribe payments.

Overall, corruption can be especially pernicious in the security sector because it creates large incentives - enabling a shadow economy to flourish in the country. Shadow economies are harmful because their opaqueness hides information about a country's economic activities, Gross Domestic Product (GDP), and real average income, impeding implementation of sound fiscal and monetary policies.

Recommendation.

1. Conduct corruption assessments as part of SSR. Draw upon the work that USAID has done in this area.

2. To improve SSR program effectiveness in a given environment, develop vignettes on corruption in the security sector and incorporate procedures to abate corruption.

3. Corruption is not an absolute in many fragile states. Much of the population may subscribe to shadow institutions and informal practices because relevant state insitutions may not exist or function properly. Thus, it is important to concentrate reforms and anti-corruption efforts on the critical institutions in the security sector - such as police, customs and border guards.

4. Fighting corruption in the security sector should be given top priority in the anti-corruption strategy within a given country, since the security sector is the major fighting force against corruption.

Implication.

Not addressing corruption in the security sector can damage the image of the state and impede the flow of investments into the country, which is the basic precondition for development.

Not addressing corruption in the security sector can result in a lack of physical security in the country and high levels of organized crime, further discouraging local and foreign investments.

Anti-corruption heavily depends on the political will of the leadership and its commitment to reform (particularly in the security sector).

Comments.

A related report which summarizes the results of the 25 Feb 2010 USIP seminar is "Fighting Corruption in Security Sector Reform," by Robert Perito and Madeline Kristoff, USIP Peace Brief 32, 20 May 2010.

Event Description.

This observation is based on the seminar "Fighting Corruption in Security Sector Reform (SSR)," 25 Feb 2010, United States Institute for Peace (USIP).

Return to
"Quick Look"

g. Topic. Strengthening Public Services in Post-conflict (603)

Observation.

Strengthening public servants' knowledge, skills, networks and attitudes is key to any improvement in government performance, because it is through public servants that services are planned and delivered.

Discussion.

The success of government in post-conflict society depends on the performance of the public service in providing critical services to the population and restoring trust and confidence in governance. This is because the public service constitutes the heartbeat of any government. Public servants pervade the entire sphere of government action. They are schoolteachers, medical practitioners, judges, court workers, police officers, military men and women, agricultural extension workers, road constructors, forestry officers, administrative officials, parliamentarians, finance officers, planners, etc. They are engaged in every facet of government activity, but most of them work directly with citizens, to whom they represent the face of government. Therefore, the quality of public servants in terms of knowledge, skills, attitudes and networks can make or break public trust in a post-conflict government.

Post-conflict public administration situations are not always similar. The public services break down in different ways, depending on the nature of the conflict and the conditions present afterwards. Consequently, countries will face different challenges in rebuilding their human resources capabilities, and experience gained in one situation may not be relevant in another. For example, in South Africa after the fall of the apartheid regime, the institutions, systems, structures and even personnel of the public service were in place and intact. However, they did not reflect South African demographics, as the white minority was vastly overrepresented.

The South African situation was different from the one in Rwanda after the 1994 genocide, when most public servants were killed. The survivors, many of whom were implicated in genocidal acts, escaped into Zaire (now the Democratic Republic of Congo) carrying files, records and other movable public service assets. When these exiles returned to Rwanda, they took over public offices in an unauthorized, uncoordinated manner. These new self-declared officials had to be removed and the vacancies filled in an orderly fashion. By the time the new regime settled in, knowledgeable and skilled personnel were unavailable, and the public service's systems and institutions, along with equipment, office space and logistics, were severely lacking.

A somewhat similar situation existed in Timor-Leste after 1999. An estimated 7,000 Indonesian civil servants had fled the Territory after Indonesian rule collapsed, and institutions and public records were destroyed or removed. This left a void throughout government because Indonesian officials had formerly occupied most of the technical and management positions. There had been limited development of Timorese skills in administration and governance. Also, whereas some of the Rwandans who returned after the genocide were eager to work and reconstruct their country, the Indonesians who fled Timor-Leste had little interest in returning. When the United Nations took over the administration of the Territory, there was no such thing as the Timor-Leste public service. Initially the United Nations had to rely on Member State volunteers, as new Timorese civil servants were being trained.

Uganda had a very different problem after the civil war that ended in 1986. Uganda's post-conflict public service was overstaffed; bloated by redundant positions with overlapping functions. The system was also plagued by poor remuneration, moonlighting, extensive corruption and uncommitted personnel. These examples illustrate the wide variation in human resource capacity in post-conflict countries. Not surprisingly, then, approaches to strengthening human resources within the public service will vary from country to country. Where a substantial number of personnel have been inherited from the outgoing regime, the task may be simply to change employees' attitudes towards the new government and towards serving the public. Such was the case in Uganda after 1986. In situations such as Rwanda, where the public service has been flooded by returning exiles without the necessary education, skills or experience, then massive immediate retraining is required, not only to transmit knowledge and skills but also to cultivate a sense of togetherness and a shared work ethic. In a situation like Timor-Leste or Kosovo, where United Nations personnel from different countries and cultures constituted an interim public service, the initial concern is to help everyone work together harmoniously in a new environment that is often insecure.

Recommendation.

1. The quality of public servants is crucial to the recovery of a post-conflict government and the trust that people have in it. This makes capacity-building in the public service essential for post-conflict recovery. Strengthening public servants' knowledge, ethics, skills, networks and attitudes is key, because it is through public servants that government services are planned and delivered, critical innovations conceived and realized, needed reforms carried out and trust in government restored.

2. The nature of the conflict, the levels of violence and destruction, and the conditions that emerge after the conflict determine the state of human resources in the public service. Reconstruction efforts must be tailored to the specific situation.

3. Reconstruction efforts should proceed from an accurate count of a country's public servants and an accurate picture of their knowledge and skills. Because employee censuses are expensive, they should be planned to fit within the overall strategy for developing human resources in the public service. In addition, censuses should be designed for congruence with the local context to ensure that the government has the capacity to effectively use the data collected.

4. It is highly desirable for oversight of the recruitment process to be managed by independent bodies such as civil service commissions to avoid cronyism, nepotism, and other forms of favoritism. But because it takes time to create and develop such institutions, interim measures need to be devised to address the immediate challenge of recruiting competent personnel. If merit-based recruitment is introduced early, there is a greater chance of limiting patronage and other harmful practices and instead ensuring a well-functioning public service.

5. Violence takes a toll on civil servants not only in terms of their numbers, but also in terms of their behavior and motivation. To rebuild the ranks of qualified personnel, it is not enough to remedy skills deficits and knowledge gaps. Efforts must also be made to restore integrity, ethics and professional conduct in the public service.

6. Diversity within the population should be reflected within the public service. If men and women, as well as members of all ethnic, religious and other groups, are actively included in the government, then conflict is less likely to erupt. A representative, merit-based, service-oriented public service can provide a model for participation, inclusive decision-making, reconciliation and social cohesion, and proactive peace-building.

7. Most post-conflict countries lack the financial resources to pay public servants adequately, and reliance on foreign aid and technical assistance is unsustainable

in the long term. Donors thus need to work strategically with post-conflict governments to help them develop pay management and incentive systems that will attract the requisite personnel without overtaxing the budget.

Implication.

The security situation will have to improve or be at a level so that public servants can conduct their work in relative safety in order to be effective. This will be important if public servants have been killed or driven off from their homeland.

Heavy external support will be needed for countries that have undergone devastating violence and upheaval. Host nation governments will likely not have the means and resources to organize, train, and mentor public service personnel following a conflict.

Foreign nations will take on many functions of government the longer it takes for host-nation public servants to fill positions in government and become proficient. People's attitudes, confidence and support in their government will be partially affected by who is actually serving their needs. The tipping point is that stage when the consensus is that their own people are serving their needs instead of foreigners.

Foreign nations will have to recognize and accept that the resulting public service may not be the one they desire because of ethnic, cultural, or social factors. The key will be to train people to professional and ethical standards.

Event Description.

This observation is based on Chapter IV "Strengthening Human Resources in the Public Service" of the report "Reconstructing Public Administration after Conflict: Challenges, Practices and Lessons Learned," United Nations Department of Economic & Social Affairs, World Public Sector Report 2010, March 2010.

Return to "Quick Look"

h. **Topic**. Reducing Judicial Corruption (USAID) (507)

Observation.

The rule of law and control of corruption are at the centerpiece for successfully addressing challenges in social, economic, and political development. Reducing corruption significantly impacts the rule of law and confidence in governmental institutions. Ultimately, people must have confidence in their system in order to accept it, use it for legal actions, and participate in improving it.

Discussion.

Judicial corruption is defined as "the abuse of entrusted authority for private gain by judges, prosecutors, public defenders, court officials, and lawyers who are intimately involved in the operation of the judicial system." Addressing judicial corruption requires attention to the broader context of corruption in the entire justice system, including law enforcement agencies and society as a whole.

Some corruption is found in the judiciaries of all countries, whether rich or poor, democratic or authoritarian. Corruption is found in all legal systems, whether state-based or non-state, formal or informal, civil law, common law, or religious law. Completely eradicating corruption is not realistic. The goal should be a judicial system that adheres to high standards of independence and impartiality, integrity, accountability, and transparency.

Judicial systems that provide timely access to fair and impartial judicial services and uphold the rule of law consistently display qualities of independence, impartiality, integrity, accountability, and transparency. Judicial systems that respect these values minimize opportunities for corruption, exercise vigilance against risks of corruption, and respond decisively to corruption when it is detected. Principal measures include transparent and merit-based selection of personnel, reasonable compensation and working conditions, simplified procedures, internal controls, reliable statistics, objective performance standards, vigorous ethical and disciplinary programs, adequate financing, public access to information, and civil society monitoring. As a result, corrupt acts are rare and isolated events. At the same time, such measures increase the system's overall efficiency, fairness, and effectiveness.

Recommendation.

A number of development organizations and NGOs have reviewed their experience in published reports that reach highly consistent conclusions and contain helpful recommendations for programming. In general, these reports reflect the following as common features of successful efforts to reduce judicial corruption:

1. Address the legal, political, social, economic and cultural context within which the judiciary operates.

    - Sustainable solutions take into account the social norms, economics, politics, institutional culture, and legal traditions of the country that can influence the supply, demand and tolerance of corruption.

    - Anticorruption efforts should not be freestanding. Rather, they should be integrated into coherent programs to strengthen the capacity and effectiveness of the judiciary and should take into account broader issues of fairness and transparency throughout the multi-institutional and multi-stakeholder justice system.

2. Rely on in-depth knowledge of the local legal system, including its history, procedures, practices, institutions, and relationships that affect the administration of justice.

- An assessment, with input from a range of experts and disciplines, should document baseline data about the justice system, including prevailing kinds of corrupt activities, key actors, and apparent causes and consequences of corruption.

- Knowledge of the system can help determine the appropriate sequencing of actions. Strengthening corrupt institutions before reforms are introduced might further entrench corruption in the judicial system. On the other hand, measures that depend on capacity (e.g., for producing accurate statistics about system performance) obviously cannot be implemented if the responsible institutions lack the necessary capacity.

- An assessment should include input from those who know the judicial system best - those who operate it (judges and court staff) and those who use it (lawyers and litigants).

3. Consider the readiness of leaders to take risks of confronting corrupt interests, the strength of motivations and incentives for change of various stakeholders, and the capacity of local institutions to implement change.

- Sustained commitment from senior levels of the judiciary and leadership by example are especially important because achieving a non-corrupt judiciary is a complex and time-consuming process. Intense opposition from vested interests is likely, and attitudes among judges accustomed to existing collegial norms are often resistant to change. (Brief tenure in key leadership positions might warrant an initial focus on creating a more sustainable environment for a long-term effort.)

- Identifiable stakeholder interests should be engaged within the public sector and civil society, including potential champions in the executive and legislative branches and in universities, law-related research and policy advocacy organizations, legal services groups, NGOs, professional and business associations, and the media.

- Demands on institutions' response for implementation need to be consistent with their capacities, usually accompanied by capacity-strengthening efforts and increasing responsibilities.

4. Give high priority to the independence of judges to decide cases on their merits, balanced by the need for judges to be accountable under high standards of integrity, productivity, and sound management of public resources.

- Judicial independence involves issues of the selection of judges, security of tenure, promotion and transfers, financial and administrative autonomy, and safeguards against interference through manipulation of budgets, salaries, or working conditions.

- Judicial accountability involves responsibility for compliance with performance standards, the applicable code of professional conduct, and established legal norms. While judges must be accountable, it is a constant challenge to find the appropriate balance so that accountability does not undermine independence.

- Even the most carefully crafted structures for independence and accountability can be abused. Beyond specific rules and procedures, these values need to be reinforced by attitudes, expectations, and continuous vigilance through transparent processes and concerned citizens.

5. Encourage a broadly participatory, locally owned program that fosters adherence to high standards of judicial integrity through sound policies, competent institutions, and transparent procedures.

- A normative framework for the judiciary should strive for clear and objective standards.

- Management practices and systems should minimize opportunities for corruption through procedures that limit possible favoritism (e.g., random case assignment, accountability for case files), standardized performance guidelines, and timely collection and analysis of data.

- Codes of ethics should be given practical vitality through educational programs, judicial mentoring and counseling, citizen complaint procedures, and investigative and disciplinary mechanisms.

- Transparency should extend to all aspects of the judicial system: selection of judges, openness of proceedings, publication of decisions, public access to information about court operations and performance, disclosure of assets and income of judges and other senior judicial officials, and civil society monitoring of judicial performance.

6. Foster harmonized international support for locally owned programs, including enhanced incentives for sustained improvement in achieving measurable results.

- Assistance programs are temporary; they should support enduring local capacity for improved performance.

- Harmonized donor support for local strategies increases prospects for sustainable development and opens possibilities for complementarities of efforts and rewards.

Implication.

Programs and assistance that do not include judiciary high standards, independence, impartiality, integrity, accountability, and transparency will not succeed in reducing judiciary corruption. Such corruption will reflect the effectiveness of governance as a whole.

An ineffective or poorly designed judicial monitoring and evaluation system will not be able to weed out corrupt personnel in the judicial system. Problems in the system will not be identified, and national stakeholders and international partners cannot evaluate progress, anticipate problems, or apply corrective measures.

The recommendations above should help to develop a good judicial system, provide timely access to fair and impartial judicial services, and uphold the rule of law in a consistent manner. Successful judicial systems should be able to minimize opportunities for corruption, be more vigilant to the risks of corruption, and respond decisively to corruption when detected.

Strengthening the judicial system will also foster public confidence in the system and rule of law. The confidence also may extend to other government institutions and bureaucrats as well. Ultimately, a strong and fair judicial system should allow people to be more participatory. A strong judicial system along with effective rule of law should also improve donor support and international assistance.

Event Description.

This observation is based on the report "Reducing Corruption in the Judiciary," June 2009, produced for review by the United States Agency for International Development. It was prepared by Mr. James Michel, Senior Counsel for DPK Consulting.

Return to

"Quick Look"

3. **CONCLUSION**

The complex nature of anti-corruption calls for civilian and military Stability Ops planners/practitioners, donor staffs, and host nation officials, to work in close cooperation in the development, implementation, and oversight of anti-corruption practices and actions.

In order to attain success in anti-corruption efforts, the following elements should be focal points for Stability Ops practitioners:

- Create an anti-corruption strategy / road map at the very outset
- Identify and assess the causes and vulnerabilities for corruption in a given post-conflict environment
- Work with a core group of stakeholders within the host nation to serve as the cornerstone for anti-corruption efforts; build alliances
- Establish anti-corruption systems in the host nation security sector – military, police, border security, etc.
- Strengthen the host nation's legal frameworks, procedures, anti-corruption ethics, and judicial accountability
- Establish reliable public finance systems in the host nation for budgeting, procurement, and tax administration
- Create accountability and tracking mechanisms – both within and outside government
- Work with host nation government officials to promote access to information on the allocation, utilization, and management of resources
- Provide training to host nation civil servants on combating corruption
- Monitor the delivery of government services to detect instances of corruption
- Work with donors on accountability and transparency
- Draw upon the anti-corruption expertise of the UNDP, USAID, and similar organizations working in the post-conflict environment
- Provide pre-deployment anti-corruption training to U.S. personnel and partners (civilian and military), along with periodic reminders while in-country
- Conduct information operations to tell the populace what is being done about corruption

Through such a comprehensive, holistic approach to anti-corruption, post-conflict countries can win the fight against corruption – as well as enhance stability and long-term economic and social development.

4. __COMMAND POC__

Lessons and content selected by Mr. Dave Mosinski, PKSOI Lessons Learned Analyst.

PKSOI reviewer:
COL Rory Radovich
Chief, Publications & Knowledge Management Div

Contact us at:
CARL_SOLLIMS@us.army.mil
Comm: 717.245.3031
DSN: 242.3031

>>>>|<<<<

 **Related Documents, References, and Links**

> USAID - Anti-corruption Assessment Handbook

> USAID - Fighting Corruption in Countries Rebuilding after Conflict

> USAID - Program Brief: Anti-corruption and Police Integrity

> USAID - Reducing Corruption in the Judiciary

> USAID - A Handbook on Fighting Corruption

> UN - Anti-Corruption Toolkit

> UNDP - Fighting Corruption in Post-Conflict and Recovery Situations: Learning from the Past

> Transparency International - Preventing Corruption in Humanitarian Operations

> Life & Peace Institute - Pilfering the Peace: The Nexus Between Corruption and Peace-building

> U4 - Anti-corruption Resource Centre

www.ingramcontent.com/pod-product-compliance
Lightning Source LLC
Chambersburg PA
CBHW081130280526
45787CB00007B/3037